Around the World in Eighty Poems

Selected by
James Berry

Illustrated by
Katherine Lucas

chronicle books · san francisco

First published in the United States in 2002 by Chronicle Books LLC.

This collection copyright © 2001 by James Berry.
Illustrations copyright © 2001 by Katherine Lucas.
All rights reserved.

Originally published in Great Britain in 2001 by Macmillan Children's Books,
a division of Macmillan Publishers Ltd.

North American text design by Kristen M. Nobles.
Typeset in Veljovic.
The illustrations in this book were rendered in acrylic paints.
Manufactured in China.

Library of Congress Cataloging-in-Publication Data available.

ISBN 0-8118-3506-5

10 9 8 7 6 5 4 3 2 1

Chronicle Books LLC
85 Second Street, San Francisco, California 94105

www.chroniclekids.com

Contents

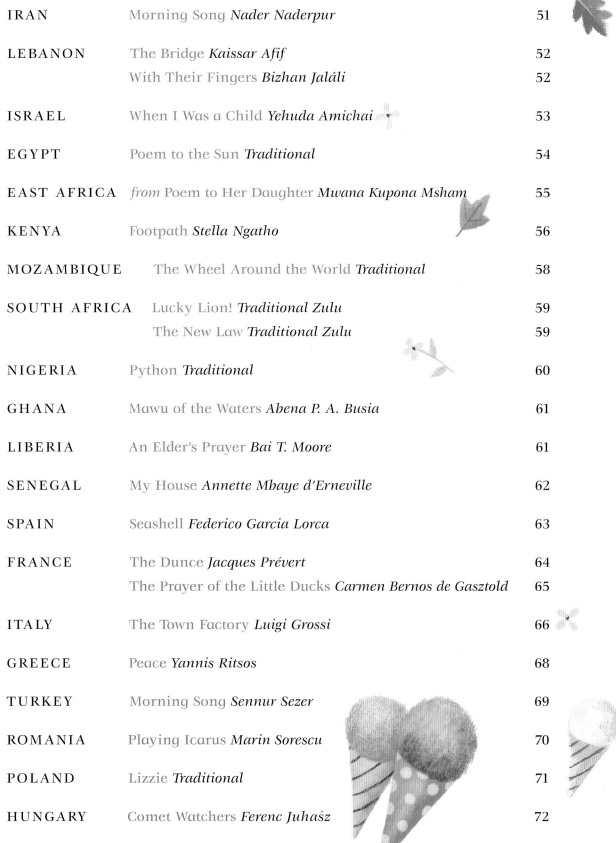

Preface

BY JAMES BERRY

More and more young people are taking to the reading and writing of poetry. Why is this? In it we discover the sense of fun in movement, the possibilities of language, the joy of word music and seeing differently.

Around the World in Eighty Poems is a contribution to this new, lively world of children's poetry. I've chosen these poems because each one in some way excites me, and I hope you will feel that excitement too. So, this travel around the world is more than just a holiday trip. It takes you into new and different experiences in different surroundings where you can share different everyday lives.

It is a reminder that we are a one-world family of people. With more information, better transportation and more flying around the world, our interest in other people and cultures simply grows. When I was a little boy in Jamaica, I hardly ever left my village. Just occasionally I went into our town, fourteen miles away. Life has given me the opportunity to travel thousands of miles from my village now and to go all over the world, and I never cease to be fascinated by different faces, different landscapes and weathers and how people live differently, together. Poetry celebrates all these differences and brings them into the pages of books so we can share them.

So, even though most of you reading this book will live in cities or built-up areas, when you read this poem by an Inuit poet, you will be able to see the animals at the end of the winter, coming down out of the forests:

> *Glorious it is to see*
> *The caribou flocking down from the forests . . .*

The poem is about change and seasons and the relief of spring. In celebrating the world and its glories, these poems find language with music in it to help create a reminder of joyful moments. As the Mexican poet Amado Nervo says:

> *Lark, let us sing!*
> *Waterfall, let us leap!*
> *Streamlet, let us run! . . .*

Poems make pictures. They are better than television. They make you see something for yourself, behind your eyes, like the picture in these lines from "Flying Fox" by Albert Wendt of New Zealand:

> *More rat than bird,*
> *more superstition than fox,*
> *you hang from that banyan . . .*

You get an immediate sense, not only of what the bat looks like, but how threatening the poet finds it. Inventive poetry finds fun everywhere. Popular poetry is full of play. More and more poetry for children works

8

with everyday language that creates rhythm and movement, like Michael Rosen's poem "Busy Day":

> *Pop in*
> *pop out*
> *pop over the road*
> *pop out for a walk*
> *pop in for a talk . . .*

Poetry makes you think. Some poems are puzzling, yet they give you strong images to work on, to get an understanding. You feel they are telling something important about your life and living. As the poet Kaissar Afif of Lebanon says:

> *Poetry is a river*
> *And solitude a bridge.*
>
> *Through writing*
> *We cross it . . .*

Perhaps the poems in this anthology will build bridges for you. This collection offers you fresh poems as new acquaintances, which I hope will become old friends.

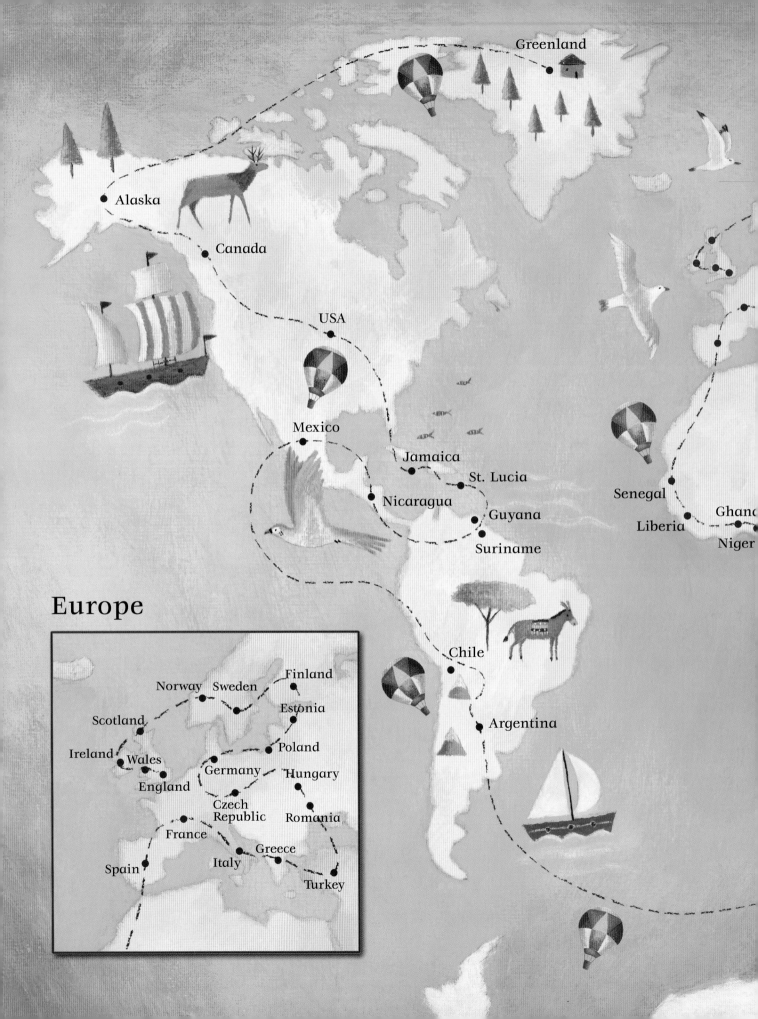

Greenland

Alaska

Canada

USA

Mexico

Jamaica

St. Lucia

Nicaragua

Guyana

Suriname

Senegal

Liberia

Ghana

Niger

Chile

Argentina

Europe

Norway   Sweden   Finland

Scotland   Estonia

Ireland   Wales

England   Germany   Poland

Hungary

Czech
Republic   Romania

France

Greece

Spain   Italy   Turkey

Glorious It Is

Glorious it is to see
The caribou flocking down from the forests
And beginning
Their wanderings to the north.
Timidly they watch
For the pitfalls of man.
Glorious it is to see
The great herds from the forests
Spreading out over plains of white.

Glorious it is to see
Early summer's short-haired caribou
Beginning to wander.
Glorious to see them trot
To and fro
Across the promontories.
Seeking for a crossing place.

Glorious it is
To see great musk oxen
Gathering in herds.
The little dogs they watch for
When they gather in herds.
Glorious to see.

Glorious it is
To see the long-haired winter caribou
Returning to the forests.
Fearfully they watch
For the little people,
While the herd follows the ebb-mark of the sea
With a storm of clattering hooves.
Glorious it is
When wandering time is come.

TRADITIONAL INUIT*
Arctic Circle

*Inuit people live in lands in and around the Arctic Circle,
such as Greenland, Canada, and Alaska.*

Ayii, Ayii, Ayii

Ayii, ayii, ayii
My arms, they wave in the air,
My hands, they flutter behind my back
They wave above my head
Like the wings of a bird.
Let me move my feet.
Let me dance.
Let me shrug my shoulders.
Let me shake my body.
Let me crouch down.
My arms, let me fold them.
Let me hold my hands under my chin.

TRADITIONAL INUIT
Arctic Circle

Spell for Catching a Bearded Seal

What smell
do I smell of?
Of the smell of a bearded seal
the smell of earth and clay

TRADITIONAL INUIT
Arctic Circle

14

Ice

was the first time
anyone remembers it happening

the fields froze
in our village
in south china

we broke some
not knowing what it was
and took it to the junk peddler

he thought it was glass
and traded us a penny
for it

he wrapped it up
in old cloth and placed it
on top of his basket

of course
the noon day sun melted it

by the time
we came back with more
he had gotten wise

JIM WONG-CHU, *Chinese-Canadian*
Canada

Could I Say I Touched You

could I say I touched you
or that this quiet brown feather that blows
in my hand is what you are
touch of fur
cry of a gliding hawk
no other way can it be
to know you as a soft, sweet rain
or the unswerving flight of an eagle on wing
thank you for beautiful thoughts
for being a part of me, somewhere in time

HAROLD LITTLEBIRD, *Laguna and Santo Domingo Pueblos*
USA

The Six-Quart Basket

The six-quart basket
    one side gone
        half the handle torn off

    sits in the center of the lawn
        and slowly fills up
            with the white fruits of the snow.

RAYMOND SOUSTER
Canada

Sundown at Darlington 1878

the children enter
to sit near the fire

we have come a long way
to this place
where the sun through grey
winter skies whispers our
names

dreams fill the sleep of the old
their voices touch the darkness
making it holy

we have come a long way

the colors of winter weigh heavy
on this worn country

there is no sound from the trees
yet at night the ghost still dances
among the horses
the dogs still
wander the river land
barking on and on
into the damp
fall wind

LANCE HENSON, *Cheyenne*
USA

17

Fifth Grade Autobiography

I was four in this photograph fishing
with my grandparents at a lake in Michigan.
My brother squats in poison ivy.
His Davy Crockett cap
sits squared on his head so the raccoon tail
flounces down the back of his sailor suit.

My grandfather sits to the far right
in a folding chair,
and I know his left hand is on
the tobacco in his pants pocket
because I used to wrap it for him
every Christmas. Grandmother's hips
bulge from the brush, she's leaning
into the ice chest, sun through the trees
printing her dress with soft
luminous paws.

I am staring jealously at my brother;
the day before he rode his first horse, alone.
I was strapped in a basket
behind my grandfather.
He smelled of lemons. He's died—

but I remember his hands.

RITA DOVE
USA

Autobiographia Literaria

When I was a child
I played by myself in a
corner of the schoolyard
all alone.

I hated dolls and I
hated games, animals were
not friendly and birds
flew away.

If anyone was looking
for me I hid behind a
tree and cried out, "I am
an orphan."

And here I am, the
centre of all beauty!
writing these poems!
Imagine!

FRANK O'HARA
USA

Trips

eeeveryyee time
when i take my bath
and comb my hair (i mean
mommy brushes it till i almost cry)
and put on my clean clothes
and they all say MY
HOW NICE YOU LOOK
and i smile and say
"thank you mommy cleaned
me up"
then i sit down and mommy says
GET UP FROM THERE YOU GONNA BE DIRTY
'FORE I HAVE A CHANCE TO GET DRESSED
MYSELF
and i want to tell her if you was
my size the dirt would catch
you up faster too

NIKKI GIOVANNI
USA

20

I, Too,
Sing America

I, too, sing America.

I am the darker brother.
They send me to eat in the kitchen
When company comes,
But I laugh,
And eat well,
And grow strong.

Tomorrow,
I'll be at the table
When company comes.
Nobody'll dare
Say to me,
"Eat in the kitchen,"
Then.

Besides,
They'll see how beautiful I am
And be ashamed—

I, too, am America.

LANGSTON HUGHES
USA

Pinda Cake

De pinda cake lady comin' down
With her basket an' glass case she comin' to town,
She stop by de school gate an' set up her stall,
An' while she a-set up, hear de ole lady bawl;

Pinda! Pinda cake!
Pinda! Pinda cake!
Gal an' bwoy me jus' done bake,
Come buy yuh lovely pinda cake!

She have grater cake an' she have duckunoo,
Coconut drops an' bulla cake too,
Jackass corn an' plantain tart,
But the t'ing dat dearest to me heart

Is pinda! Pinda cake!
Pinda! Pinda cake!
Gal an' bwoy me jus' done bake,
Come buy yuh lovely pinda cake!

We all crowd round her an' yuh can tell
By de look o' de cake dem, an' de spicy smell
Dat they won't stay in de glass case fe too long,
As we buy from de lady, we join in de song.

Pinda! Pinda cake!
Pinda! Pinda cake!
Gal an' bwoy me jus' done bake,
Come buy yuh lovely pinda cake!

VALERIE BLOOM
Jamaica

Jamaican Song

Little toad little toad mind yourself
mind yourself let me plant my corn
plant my corn to feed my horse
feed my horse to run my race—
the sea is full of more than I know
moon is bright like night time sun
night is dark like all eyes shut
    Mind—mind yu not harmed
    somody know bout yu
    somody know bout yu

Little toad little toad mind yourself
mind yourself let me build my house
build my house to be at home
be at home till I one day vanish—
the sea is full of more than I know
moon is bright like night time sun
night is dark like all eyes shut
    Mind—mind yu not harmed
    somody know bout yu
    somody know bout yu

JAMES BERRY
Jamaica

24

Mango

On Sunday afternoons in mango season,

Alleyne would fill his enamel basin

with golden-yellow fruit, wash them in clean water,

then sit out in the yard, under the grapefruit tree,

near the single rose bush, back to the crotons,

place the basin between his feet,

and slowly eat his mangoes, one by one, down to the clean white seed.

His felt-hat was always on his head. The yellow basin, chipped near the bottom,

with its thin green rim, the clear water, the golden fruit,

him eating slowly, carefully, picking the mango fiber from his teeth,

under those clear, quiet afternoons, I remember.

Me sitting in the doorway of my room, one foot on the steps that dropped

into the yard, reading him, over a book. That's how it was.

ROBERT LEE
St. Lucia

25

Realarro

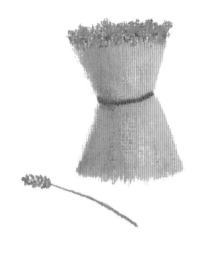

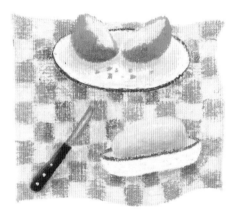

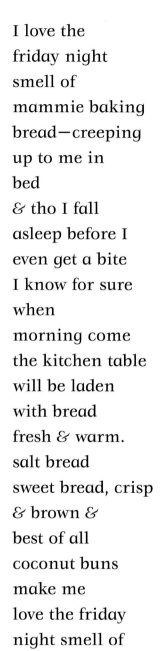

I love the
friday night
smell of
mammie baking
bread—creeping
up to me in
bed
& tho I fall
asleep before I
even get a bite
I know for sure
when
morning come
the kitchen table
will be laden
with bread
fresh & warm.
salt bread
sweet bread, crisp
& brown &
best of all
coconut buns
make me
love the friday
night smell of

mammie baking bread
putting me to bed
to sleep
dreaming

MARC MATTHEWS
Guyana

Snow-cone

Snow-cone nice
Snow-cone sweet
Snow-cone is crush ice
and good for the heat.

When sun really hot
and I thirsty a lot,
Me alone,
Yes me alone,
could eat ten snow-cone.

If you think is lie I tell
wait till you hear the snow-cone bell,
wait till you hear the snow-cone bell.

JOHN AGARD
Guyana

Sea Timeless Song

Hurricane come
and hurricane go
but sea—sea timeless
sea timeless
sea timeless
sea timeless
sea timeless

Hibiscus bloom
then dry wither so
but sea—sea timeless
sea timeless
sea timeless
sea timeless
sea timeless

Tourist come
and tourist go
but sea—sea timeless
sea timeless
sea timeless
sea timeless
sea timeless

GRACE NICHOLS
Guyana

One Tree

one tree
so many leaves
one tree

one river
so many creeks
all are going to one sea

one head
so many thoughts
thoughts among which one good one
must be

one god
so many ways of worshiping
but one father

one Suriname
so many hair types
so many skin colors
so many tongues
one people

DOBRU RAVALES
Suriname

Sonatina

The princess is sad . . . What can be wrong with the princess?
Sighs escape from her strawberry lips
which have lost their laughter, which have lost their color.
The princess is pale on her chair of gold,
the keyboard of her sonorous harpsichord is silent;
and in a vase there droops a forgotten flower.

RUBÉN DARÍO
Nicaragua

Rocking

The sea its thousands of waves
divinely rocks.
Listening to the loving seas,
I rock my child.

The wind wandering in the night
rocks the fields of wheat.
Listening to the loving winds,
I rock my child.

God in Heaven His thousands of worlds
rocks without noise.
Feeling His hand in the dark,
I rock my child.

GABRIELA MISTRAL
Chile

31

The Ombú

Each region on earth
has a prominent feature;
Brazil, its burning sun,
Peru, mines of silver;
Montevideo, its hill;
Buenos Aires—beautiful fatherland—
has the majestic pampas,
and the pampas have the ombú.*

LUIS L. DOMÍNGUEZ
Argentina
* *The ombú is a kind of tree.*

Solidarity

Lark, let us sing!
Waterfall, let us leap!
Streamlet, let us run!
Diamond, let us shine!
Eagle, let us fly!
Dawn, let us be born!
    To sing!
    To leap!
    To run!
    To shine!
    To fly!
    To be born!

AMADO NERVO
Mexico

Flying Fox

More rat than bird,
more superstition than fox,
you hang from that banyan
branch like a deflated black
umbrella, and when you flap
through the sky across a waxen
moon and the dead rise up
to haunt me, you're more
real than Batman.

With your razor-sharp teeth
you eat the ripe mangoes
and pawpaw in my plantation,
but wait until I catch you:
I'm going to skin you, gut you,
roast you and eat you.
I'll enjoy the eating because
I'll be chewing Batman,
Count Dracula and all superstitions
about vampires.

ALBERT WENDT
New Zealand

34

Jarrangulli

Hear that tree-lizard singin' out,
Jarrangulli.
He's singin' out for rain.
He's in a hole up in that tree.
He wants the rain to fill that hole right up
an' cover him with rain.
That water will last him till
the drought comes on again.

It's comin' dry when he sings out,
Jarrangulli.
Soon as ever he sings out,
Jarrangulli,
he's sure to bring the rain.
That feller, he's the real rain-lizard.
He's just the same as them black cockatoos,
they're the fellers for the rain.

He's deadly poison. He's
Jarrangulli.
He'll bite you sure enough.
You climb that tree an' put your hand
over that hole, he'll bite you sure enough.
He's black an' painted with white stripes.
Jarrangulli.
He's singin' out for rain.

ROLAND ROBINSON
Australia

35

Night Herons

It was after a day's rain:
the street facing the west
was lit with growing yellow;
the black road gleamed.

First one child looked and saw
and told another.
Face after face, the windows
flowered with eyes.

It was like a long fuse lighted,
the news traveling.
No one called out loudly;
everyone said "Hush."

The light deepened; the wet road
answered in daffodil colors,
and down its center
walked the two tall herons.

Stranger than wild birds, even,
what happened on those faces:
suddenly believing in something,
they smiled and opened.

Children thought of fountains,
circuses, swans feeding:
women remembered words
spoken when they were young.

Everyone said "Hush";
no one spoke loudly;
but suddenly the herons
rose and were gone. The light faded.

JUDITH WRIGHT
Australia

Ringneck Parrots

The ringneck parrots, in scattered flocks,
The ringneck parrots are screaming in their upward flight.

The ringneck parrots are a cloud of wings;
The shell parrots are a cloud of wings.

Let the shell parrots come down to rest,
Let them come down to rest on the ground!

Let the caps fly off the scented blossoms!
Let the blooms descend to the ground in a shower!

The clustering bloodwood blooms are falling down,
The clustering bloodwood blossoms, nipped by birds.

The clustering bloodwood blooms are falling down,
The clustering bloodwood blossoms, one by one.

TRADITIONAL ARANDA
Australia

Sun and Shade

Sun you are beautiful, oh beautiful,
you give us warm sunshine,
we love you so much, oh sunshine.
Shade you clumsy nonsense go away,
nobody loves you,
everybody hates you.

Shade you are beautiful, oh beautiful—
and cool.
We love you so much.
Sunshine you clumsy nonsense go away,
Nobody loves you,
everybody hates you,
shade cool shade, oh come.

MICHAEL MONDO
Papua New Guinea

39

On My Short-Sightedness

To my short-sighted eyes
The world seems better far
Than artificial aid
To sight would warrant it:
The earth is just as green,
The sky a paler blue;
Many a blurred outline
Of overlapping hue;
Shapes, forms are indistinct;
Distance a mystery;
Often a common scene
Conceals a new beauty;
Ugliness is hidden
In a curtain of mist;
And hard, cruel faces
Lose their malignity.
So do not pity me
For my short-sighted eyes;
They see an unknown world
Of wonder and surprise.

PREM CHAYA
Thailand

By Chance I Walk...

By chance I walk into the western courtyard.
There in the shelter of the porch
A solitary orchid has flowered.
How quickly the news gets around
For already the bees are arriving.

YÜAN MEI
China

Isn't It...

Isn't it true that mothers everywhere
Love to nag?
Don't do this, don't do that,
Scolding without stop.

Every morning when Mom goes to work
How happy my sister and I are!
Yet when she's late coming home from work
We rush to the curb and wait and wait...

KE YAN
China

41

The Ferryboat and the Traveler

I am a ferryboat. A traveler, you tread on me
with muddy shoes. I take you aboard to cross
the river. With you held in my arms, I go across
the currents, deep, shallow or rapid.
If you do not turn up, I await you from dawn
to dusk, despite the wind, rain or snow.
Yet, once you've crossed the river, you do not
look back on me. But I believe you will be coming
back some day.
I grow old and worn out waiting for you
day after day.
I am a ferryboat. You are a traveler.

HAN YONG-UN
Korea

An Old Temple

Goaded by drowsiness
while beating a wooden prayer bell

A handsome boy monk
has dropped off to sleep.

Buddha smiles,
Silent.

The road leads ten thousand *li* to the west.

Under the flaming evening glow
peony petals are falling.

CHIHUN CHO
Korea

Voice and Wings

Water said to Clouds: I was once clouds myself,
with huge wings like yours.

Clouds said to Water: I was once water myself,
with a clear singing voice like yours.

KINOSHITA YŪJI
Japan

Secret

When it is time for the little boy to go to bed
He runs naked and laughing through the house
Like a bird escaped from its cage
Or a prince sprung out of a magic box.
He runs stamping his bare feet around the house,
Bumping his head, banging his hands or his bottom
On anything that stands in his way—on the sliding doors
Of paper, on the walls—rejoicing in the feel of the cool air.

His mother is chasing after him with his little pajamas.
A little boy naked is skinny as a water sprite—
He is driven into a corner at last, and
Waits there breathlessly, pressing himself against the wall,
So very tiny he looks, with his face to the wall.
Then his mother catches him and quickly covers him up
As if they shared a secret no one else must know.

SENKE MOTOMARO
Japan

44

A Kiss on the Head

A kiss on the head—wipes away misery.
I kiss your head.

A kiss on the eyes—takes away sleeplessness.
I kiss your eyes.

A kiss on the lips—quenches the deepest thirst.
I kiss your lips.

A kiss on the head—wipes away memory.
I kiss your head.

MARINA TSVETAEVA
Russia

Bicycles

The bicycles lie
In the woods, in the dew.
    Between the birch trees
    The highway gleams.

They fell, fell down
Mudguard to mudguard,
    Handlebar to handlebar
    Pedal to pedal.

And you can't
Wake them up!
    Petrified monsters,
    Their chains entwined.

Huge and surprised
They stare at the sky.
    Above them, green dusk
    Resin, and bumblebees.

In the luxurious
Rustling of chamomile, peppermint
    Leaves they lie. Forgotten,
    Asleep. Asleep.

ANDREI VOZNESENSKY
Russia

The Stars

When night comes
I stand on the stairway and listen,
the stars are swarming in the garden
and I am standing in the dark.
Listen, a star fell with a tinkle!
Do not go out on the grass with bare feet;
my garden is full of splinters.

EDITH SÖDERGRAN
Finland

Love and Music

He comes from the house as lightning flickers in the sky
His hair is tied in a knot on one side
He stands shining in the court
What is he doing standing in the court?
What is the boy doing? He is shining like the lightning
He is standing on tiptoe playing on the flute
He leaps in the air as he beats on his drum
Come, let us go and listen to his flute.

TRADITIONAL GOND
India

47

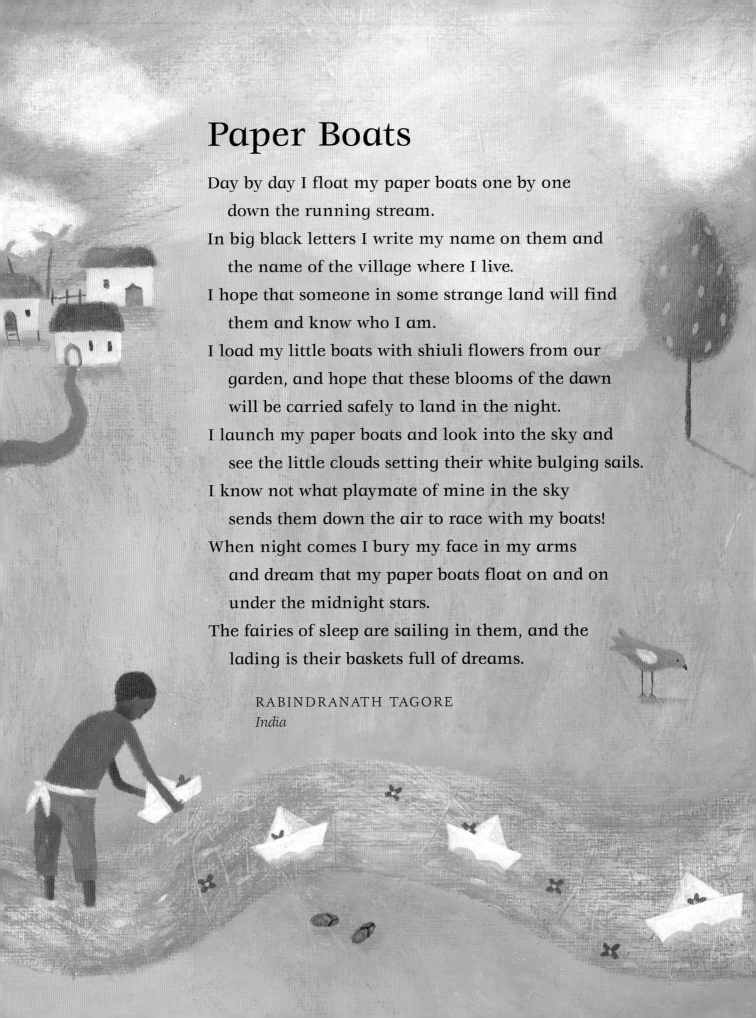

Paper Boats

Day by day I float my paper boats one by one
    down the running stream.
In big black letters I write my name on them and
    the name of the village where I live.
I hope that someone in some strange land will find
    them and know who I am.
I load my little boats with shiuli flowers from our
    garden, and hope that these blooms of the dawn
    will be carried safely to land in the night.
I launch my paper boats and look into the sky and
    see the little clouds setting their white bulging sails.
I know not what playmate of mine in the sky
    sends them down the air to race with my boats!
When night comes I bury my face in my arms
    and dream that my paper boats float on and on
    under the midnight stars.
The fairies of sleep are sailing in them, and the
    lading is their baskets full of dreams.

RABINDRANATH TAGORE
India

Holding On

I do not know if he was a sage,
nor if he was a philosopher.
I only know that he sat crosslegged,
silent on the sand by the river.

"Tell me the meaning of life," I begged.
He smiled and answered me not a word.
"I'll not leave empty-handed," I said.
He smiled and I wondered if he heard.

Exasperated I made to go
when he smiled and gathered me up some sand.
As he turned and looked into my eyes,
he let it trickle from his hand.

Uncertainly I pulled out my purse.
(Had he somehow answered after all?)
Hesitant, I gave a rupee note.
He smiled and slowly let it fall.

DEBJANI CHATTERJEE
India

Touching

This is a song
about touch and touching.
You touch me—a way of feeling.
I touch you—a way of understanding.
We are touched
by a film or a book.
We are touched
when a stranger is kind.
How can we live
without touching and being touched?

There is a healing touch,
it makes the sick whole again.
Let's keep in touch
we say to a friend who's going away.
To have the right touch
means to know how it's done.
Touching is an art,
it's the movement
to and from the heart.

Some are easily touched.
Some are hard to touch.
You are often touched.
I am often touched.

NISSIM EZEKIEL
Pakistan

50

Morning Song

In the shy blue sky
A bird cried:
"Where is it, then?
Where is the Morning?"
"It is on your wings,"
I said in reply.

And the bird flew away;
    and the Morning bloomed
    in my eyes.

NADER NADERPUR
Iran

The Bridge

Poetry is a river
And solitude a bridge.

Through writing
    We cross it,
Through reading

We return.

KAISSAR AFIF
Lebanon

With Their
Fingers

With their fingers
The trees write on the sky
Something which they repeat
        With their roots in the soil;
        They speak of happiness.

BIZHAN JALÂLI
Lebanon

When I Was a Child

When I was a child
grasses and masts stood at the seashore,
and as I lay there
I thought they were all the same
because all of them rose into the sky above me.

Only my mother's words went with me
like a sandwich wrapped in rustling waxpaper,
and I didn't know when my father would come back
because there was another forest beyond the clearing.

Everything stretched out a hand,
a bull gored the sun with its horns,
and in the nights the light of the streets caressed
my cheeks along with the walls,
and the moon, like a large pitcher, leaned over
and watered my thirsty sleep.

YEHUDA AMICHAI
Israel

53

Poem to the Sun

All the cattle are resting in the fields,
The trees and the plants are growing,
The birds flutter above the marshes,
Their wings uplifted in adoration,
And all the sheep are dancing,
All winged things are flying,
They live when you have shone on them.

The boats sail upstream and downstream alike,
Every highway is open because you dawn.
The fish in the river leap up in front of you,
Your rays are in the middle of the great green sea.

TRADITIONAL
Egypt

from Poem to Her Daughter

Daughter, take this amulet

tie it with cord and caring

I'll make you a chain of coral and pearl

to glow on your neck. I'll dress you nobly.

A gold clasp too—fine, without flaw

to keep with you always.

When you bathe, sprinkle perfume,

   and weave your hair in braids.

String jasmine for the bedspread.

Wear your clothes like a bride,

for your feet anklets, bracelets for your arms . . .

Don't forget rosewater,

don't forget henna for the palms of your hands.

MWANA KUPONA MSHAM
East Africa

Footpath

Path-let . . . leaving home, leading out,
Return my mother to me.
The sun is sinking and darkness coming,
Hens and cocks are already inside and babies drowsing,
Return my mother to me.
We do not have firewood and I have not seen the lantern,
There is no more food and the water has run out,
Path-let I pray you, return my mother to me.
Path of the hillocks, path of the small stones,
Path of slipperiness, path of the mud,
Return my mother to me.
Path of the papyrus, path of the rivers,
Path of the small forests, path of the reeds,
Return my mother to me.

Path that winds, path of the shortcut,
Over-trodden path, newly made path,
  Return my mother to me.
    Path, I implore you, return my mother to me.
     Path of the crossways, path that branches off,
      Path of the stinging shrubs, path of the bridge,
    Return my mother to me.
  Path of the open, path of the valley,
Path of the steep climb, path of the downward slope,
Return my mother to me.
Children are drowsing about to sleep,
Darkness is coming and there is no firewood,
And I have not found the lantern:
Return my mother to me.

STELLA NGATHO
Kenya

The Wheel Around the World

If all the world's children
wanted to play holding hands
they could happily make
a wheel around the sea.

If all the world's children
wanted to play holding hands
they could be sailors
and build a bridge across the seas.

What a beautiful chorus we would make
singing around the earth
if all the humans in the world
wanted to dance holding hands!

TRADITIONAL
Mozambique

Lucky Lion!

It sleeps by day!
How blessed it is,
Lion.

TRADITIONAL ZULU
South Africa

The New Law

Come here my beloved,
Come, give me a kiss.
There is a new law
Which says we must embrace each other.

TRADITIONAL ZULU
South Africa

Python

Swaggering prince
giant among snakes.
They say python has no house.
I heard it a long time ago
and I laughed and laughed and laughed.
For who owns the ground under the lemon grass?
Who owns the ground under the elephant grass?
Who owns the swamp—father of rivers?
Who owns the stagnant pool—father of waters?

Because they never walk hand in hand
people say that snakes only walk singly.
But just imagine
suppose the viper walks in front
the green mamba follows
and the python creeps rumbling behind—
who will be brave enough
to wait for them?

TRADITIONAL
Nigeria

Mawu of the Waters

With mountains as my footstool
  and stars in my curls
I reach down to reap the waters with my fingers
and look! I cup lakes in my palms.
I fling oceans around me like a shawl
and am transformed
into a waterfall.
Springs flow through me
and spill rivers at my feet
as fresh streams surge to make seas.

ABENA P. A. BUSIA
Ghana

An Elder's Prayer

O Great spirit of my forest,
I have nothing in my hand
But a chicken and some rice,
It's the gift of all my land.
    Bring us sunshine with the rains
    So the harvest moon may blow,
    Save my people from all pains;
    When the harvest time is done
    We will make a feast to you.

BAI T. MOORE
Liberia

61

My House

I have built my house

Without sand, without water

My mother's heart

Forms a great wall

My father's arms

The floor and the roof

My sister's laughter

The doors and the windows

My brother's eyes

Light up the house

My home feels good

My home is sweet

ANNETTE MBAYE D'ERNEVILLE
Senegal

62

Seashell

They've brought me a seashell.

Inside it sings
a map of the sea.
My heart
fills up with water,
with smallish fish
of shade and silver.

They've brought me a seashell.

FEDERICO GARCIA LORCA
Spain

The Dunce

He says no with his head
but his heart says yes
he says yes to what he likes
he says no to the teacher
he is on his feet
to be questioned
to be asked all the problems
suddenly he shakes with uncontrollable mirth
and he rubs them all out
the figures and the words
the dates and the names
the sentences and the traps
and despite the threats from the master
amid the jeers of the child prodigies
with all the colored chalks
upon the miserable blackboard
he draws the face of happiness.

JACQUES PRÉVERT
France

The Prayer of the Little Ducks

Dear God,

give us a flood of water.

Let it rain tomorrow and always.

Give us plenty of little slugs

and other luscious things to eat.

Protect all folk who quack

and everyone who knows how to swim.

Amen

CARMEN BERNOS DE GASZTOLD
France

65

The Town Factory

Is there such a thing
As a factory that makes towns?

Of course there is, and this is how it makes them:
With mountains and gardens and lots of streets;
And the smoke from the factory chimneys
Goes straight up in stripes—
Yellow, vermilion red,
Green, orange,
Amethyst . . .
And it tastes like fruit salad.
And everyone says, "What beautiful smoke,
and what a lovely smell!"

Yes, but what about the car fumes?

Ah, they are the color of flowers
And they smell as sweet!

Are these towns very expensive?

No, but if you want one by the sea
Then (even you will understand)
It will cost you rather more.

LUIGI GROSSI
Italy

Peace

Peace is the odor of food in the evening,
when the halting of a car in the street is not fear,
when a knock on the door means a friend

Peace is a glass of warm milk
and a book in front of the child who awakens

YANNIS RITSOS
Greece

Morning Song

Listen!
The morning has three doors in the sky.
One of them is hope.
Take it and give it to the child
let him grow with it
let him grow tall and walk tall.

Listen, listen!
The morning has three doors in the sky.
One of them is the daily bread
shining in your hands.
Let it shine on and increase
all the bright way long.

Listen, I say, listen!
The morning has three doors to the sky.
One of them is fear.
Silence it!
The bread is yours, the hope is yours.
What can fear do
when hands can speak unto other hands?

SENNUR SEZER
Turkey

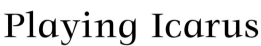

Playing Icarus

I went begging to the birds
And each of them gave me
A feather.

A high one from the vulture,
A red one from the bird of paradise,
A green one from the hummingbird,
A talking one from the parrot,
A shy one from the ostrich—
Oh, what wings I've made for myself.

I've attached them to my soul
And I've started to fly.
High flight of the vulture,
Red flight of the bird of paradise,
Green flight of the hummingbird,
Talking flight of the parrot,
Shy flight of the ostrich—
Oh, how I've flown!

MARIN SORESCU
Romania

Lizzie

Lizzie Lizzie, spinning top,
Ever dancing, never stop.
Dancing in the morning dew,
Barefoot tap, one two, one two.

Lizzie Lizzie, spinning top,
Ever dancing, never stop.
Dancing in the sun's warm rays,
Shining brightly at midday.

TRADITIONAL
Poland

Comet Watchers

One blind-calm summer night
someone tapped at the window of our house—
"Come out! Come out!
There's a miracle! There, in the sky!"

We jumped out of bed. What is it?
Some secret message from the stars?
I grabbed my mother's hand, it was warm,
I felt her heart beat in my palm.

Barefooted, in shirts and underpants
the whole village gathered out there in the cold;
scared old women, sleep-white faces
frozen in the white light of another world.

The poor came crowding into the street.
Women crossed their arms over their breasts.
Their knees shook as they gaped at the sky—
a fairy tale, a holy prophecy!

Over the hill, the star-freaked sky
blazed brighter than burning hay—
a stallion with wings and a diamond mane,
a mane of fire, a streaming tail of blood.

I gripped my mother's hand like roots.
I remember the warmth of her body still,
and father pointing up at the horse
blazing away in the fires of its own sweat.

Proudly it flew away over the roofs.
We stood, still as gravestones in its fierce light.
The sky was much darker when it had gone.
O fate of comets, will o' the wisp, our hope!

FERENC JUHÁSZ
Hungary

The Door

Go and open the door.
　Maybe outside there's
　a tree, or a wood,
　a garden,
　or a magic city.

Go and open the door.
　Maybe a dog's rummaging.
　Maybe you'll see a face,
or an eye,
or the picture
　　　　of a picture.

Go and open the door.
　If there's a fog
　it will clear.

Go and open the door.
  Even if there's only
    the darkness ticking,
    even if there's only
    the hollow wind,
    even if
        nothing
                is there,
go and open the door.

At least
there'll be
a draft.

MIROSLAV HOLUB
Czech Republic

75

Traveling in a Comfortable Car

Traveling in a comfortable car
Down a rainy road in the country
We saw a ragged fellow at nightfall
Signal to us for a ride, with a low bow.
We had a roof and we had room and we drove on
And we heard me say, in a peevish voice: No
We can't take anyone with us.
We had gone on a long way, perhaps a day's march
When suddenly I was shocked by this voice of mine
This behavior of mine and this
Whole world.

BERTOLT BRECHT
Germany

The Scarecrow

The ravens croaked: Caw, caw, caw, caw!
Who's that we saw? Who's that we saw?
We're not afraid, we're not afraid,
of such a silly masquerade!

We know, the ravens said, and smiled,
you're neither woman, man, nor child.
You can't move off and walk away.
In wind and weather there you stay.

You're just two sticks, a coat, a hat.
You think we are afraid of that?
So caw, caw, caw!

CHRISTIAN MORGENSTERN
Germany

Chant for a Child Who Is Hurt

(to be said over and over while rubbing the hurt spot)

Take the cow to the field
Fetch some hay for the cow
Squeeze milk from the cow
Bring the milk to your mom
Take bread from your mom
Give the bread to the chief
Take a coat from the chief
Send the coat to the king
Gain a cane from the king
Lead the cow with the cane
Take the cow to the field etc…

TRADITIONAL
Estonia

The Pan and the Potatoes

Phew!
I'm sweating and steaming
I feel like screaming
I'm bubbling and seething
I'm rattling like tea-things
the pan said—
took his hat off his head—and

          Phew!

I'm absolutely boiling
I'm bristling and whistling
and hustling and moiling
and all hot and sizzling
it's a mad mad bustle
the pan said—
took its hat off its head—and

                  Phew!

Ouch this hoppity, hoppity, hoppity
shouted the potatoes, popping up fit to split
no way of stopping it, dropping it, swapping it
dancing a polka, have to, dance, dancing a polka
got to go higher now, shoes are on fire now
galloping, galloping, off at a lollop
jumping and jumping and off at a wallop
turning and thumping, thumping and turning
oh this knocking and bumping and socking
off again copping it, hopping it, whopping it
makes me spit—
no way of stopping it

               KIRSI KUNNAS
               Finland

Nightmare

I never say his name aloud

and don't tell anybody

I always close all the drawers

and look behind the door before I go to bed

I cross my toes and count to eight

and turn the pillow over three times

Still he comes sometimes

one two three

like a shot

glaring at me with his eyes,

grating with his nails

and sneering his big sneer—

the Scratch Man

Uh-oh, now I said his name!

Mama, I can't sleep!

SIV WIDERBERG
Sweden

Rain

One is one, and two is two—
we sing in huddles,
we hop in puddles.
Plip, plop,
we drip on rooftop,
trip, trop,
the rain will not stop.
Rain, rain, rain, rain,
bucketing rain,
chucketing rain,
rain, rain, rain, rain,
wonderfully raw,
wet to the core!
One is one, and two is two—
we sing in huddles,
we hop in puddles.
Plip, plop,
we drip on rooftop,
trip, trop,
the rain will not stop.

SIGBJØRN OBSTFELDER
Norway

A Boy's Song

Where the pools are bright and deep,
Where the grey trout lies asleep,
Up the river and o'er the lea,
That's the way for Billy and me.

Where the blackbird sings the latest,
Where the hawthorn blooms the sweetest,
Where the nestlings chirp and flee,
That's the way for Billy and me.

Where the mowers mow the cleanest,
Where the hay lies thick and greenest;
There to trace the homeward bee,
That's the way for Billy and me.

Where the hazel bank is steepest,
Where the shadow falls the deepest,
Where the clustering nuts fall free,
That's the way for Billy and me.

Why the boys should drive away
Little sweet maidens from the play,
Or love to banter and fight so well,
That's the thing I never could tell.

But this I know, I love to play,
Through the meadow, among the hay,
Up the water and o'er the lea,
That's the way for Billy and me.

JAMES HOGG
Scotland

Two Carla Johnsons

People don't understand: there are two Carla Johnsons.
The one with wings and the one with hands.
The one who flies and the one who flops exams.
The one who goes to Alaska, to Alabama.
And the one who lives in a high-rise tower.

Two Carlas: one whose wings are sugar paper.
One whose stomach sticks out from a hernia.
One soars through rainbows; one looks out windows.
One who constantly dreams of the other Carla
who has a nicer nose better clothes and good hair.

Good hair that changes color with temper.
So if she is sad it is blue, if she is happy
it is black, if she is mad it is bright red.
Two Carlas; the one who talks a strange tongue
that nobody but the other Carla can understand.

Often Carla sits in her tower laughing at jokes.
Till the stars fall down. Till the trees dance.
Till her curtains open and close themselves.
All because the one with the wings is so funny.
So funny that both Carlas hold their tummy.

JACKIE KAY
Scotland

All the Dogs

You should have seen him—
he stood in the park and whistled,
underneath an oak tree,
and all the dogs came bounding up
and sat around him,
keeping their big eyes on him,
tails going like pendulums.
And there was one cocker pup
who went and licked his hand,
and a Labrador who whimpered
till the rest joined in.
Then he whistled a second time,
high-pitched as a stoat,
over all the shouted dog names
and whistles of owners,
till a flurry of paws
brought more dogs, panting,
as if they'd come miles,
and these too found space
on the flattened grass
to stare at the boy's
unmemorable face
which all the dogs found special.

MATTHEW SWEENEY
Ireland

What a View

What a view he has
of our town, riding
inland, the seagull!

Rows of shining roofs
and cars, the dome of
a church, or a bald-

headed farmer, and
a thousand gutters
flowing under the

black assembly
of chimneys! . . .

He would be lost,
my seagull, to see
why the names on

one side of the street
(MacAteer, Carney)
are Irish and ours

and the names across
(Carnew, MacCrea)
are English and theirs

but he would understand
the charred, sad stump
of the factory chimney

which will never burn
his tail feathers as
he perches on it

and if a procession,
Orange or Hibernian,
came stepping through

he would hear the
same thin, scrannel
note, under the drums.

And when my mother
puts her nose out
once, up and down

the narrow street,
and retires inside,
like the lady in

the weather clock,
he might well see
her point. There are

few pickings here,
for a seagull, so
far inland. A last

salute on the flag
pole of the British
Legion Hut, and he

flaps away, the
small town sinking
into its caul

of wet, too well
hedged, hillocky
Tyrone grassland.

JOHN MONTAGUE
Ireland

In the Barn

In the old oak beam
is the rustling forest

In the fork of the roof
is the pigeon's nest

In the mound of hay
is the summer meadow

In the web-winged bat
is the flittering shadow

In the fox and the owl
are the night-bringers

In the gaps between stones
are the wind's fingers

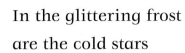
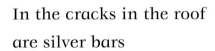

In the glittering frost
are the cold stars

In the cracks in the roof
are silver bars

In the puddle on the floor
is the moon's face

In the thawing stream
is spring's voice

In the creak of the door
is the swallow's cry

In the hole in the shutter
is the sun's eye

GILLIAN CLARKE
Wales

Busy Day

Pop in
pop out
pop over the road
pop out for a walk
pop in for a talk
pop down to the shop
can't stop
got to pop

got to pop?

pop where?
pop what?

well
I've got to
pop round
pop up
pop in to town
pop out and see
pop in for tea
pop down to the shop
can't stop
got to pop

90

got to pop?

pop where?
pop what?

well
I've got to
pop in
pop out
pop over the road
pop out for a walk
pop in for a talk . . .

MICHAEL ROSEN
England

91

Dear Mum,

while you were out
a cup went and broke itself,
a crack appeared in the blue vase
your great-great grandad
brought back from China.
Somehow, without me even turning on the tap,
the sink mysteriously overflowed.
A strange jam-stain,
about the size of a boy's hand,
appeared on the kitchen wall.
I don't think we will ever discover
exactly how the cat
managed to turn on the washing machine
(specially from the inside),
or how the self-raising flour
managed to self-raise.
I can tell you I was scared when,
as if by magic,
a series of muddy footprints
appeared on the new white carpet.
I was being good
(honest)
but I think the house is haunted so,
knowing you're going to have a fit,
I've gone over to Gran's for a bit.

BRIAN PATTEN
England

Going Out with Mum

"Still got the umbrella Dad gave me last Christmas.
Just fetch my gloves dear, no, the leather ones,
The ones I went to Baker Street to collect
And the man said 'All change' and wouldn't let me stop
To think if I had everything.
Look in the other drawer. Have you seen my purse, John?
I know I had it. I'd just paid the milkman
And the phone rang. Look in the bathroom then.
Keys, money, letters. Have you got handkerchiefs?
Don't sniff, Bridget, blow. I must make sure
I've got the address right. D'you think you'd better take macs?
Just put the bread knife away dear, you never know
Who may get in and if they see one handy
It might—no, leave the kitchen window
There's the cat."

We round the corner as the bus pulls off
From the bus stop. "Now if you'd been ready
We might have caught that. It would have made all the difference.
There might not be another one for hours."

We almost believe it's true it was our fault:
Mum's too good at being efficient for it to be hers.

JENNY JOSEPH
England

I Am the Song

I am the song that sings the bird.
I am the leaf that grows the land.
I am the tide that moves the moon.
I am the stream that halts the sand.
I am the cloud that drives the storm.
I am the earth that lights the sun.
I am the fire that strikes the stone.
I am the clay that shapes the hand.
I am the word that speaks the man.

CHARLES CAUSLEY
England

Index

Acknowledgements

The publishers wish to thank the following for permission to use copyright material:

Kaissar Afif, 'The Bridge' translated by Mansour Ajami, included in *The Space Between Our Footsteps: Poems and Paintings from the Middle East,* selected by Naomi Shihab Nye, Simon & Schuster for Young Readers, by permission of Mansour Alami; **John Agard,** 'Snow-cone' from *I Din Do Nuttin,* Bodley Head (1983), by permission of Random House UK; **Yehuda Amichai,** 'When I Was a Child' from *The Selected Poetry of Yehuda Amichai,* translated and edited by Chana Bloch and Stephen Mitchell (1996). Copyright © 1996 The Regents of the University of California, by permission of University of Calfornia Press; **James Berry,** 'Jamaican Song' from *When I Dance* by James Berry, Puffin (1990). Copyright © James Berry 1990, by permission of The Peters Fraser and Dunlop Group Ltd on behalf of the author; **Valerie Bloom,** 'Pinda Cake' from *Let Me Touch The Sky* by Valerie Bloom, Macmillan Children's Books (2000), by permission of the author; **Bertolt Brecht,** 'Travelling in a Comfortable Car' from *Poems 1913-1956* by Bertolt Brecht, translated by Michael Hamburger, by permission of Methuen Publishing Ltd; **Charles Causley,** 'I am the Song' from *Collected Poems for Children 1951-2000,* Macmillan (2000), by permission of David Higham Associates on behalf of the author; **Debjani Chatterjee,** 'Holding On', first published in *I Was That Woman,* Hippopotamus Press (1989), by permission of the author; **Prem Chaya,** 'On My Short-Sightedness' from *Span, An Adventure in Asian and Australian Writing,* Frank Cheshire Publishing Pty Ltd, by permission of Pearson Education; **Chihun Cho,** 'An Old Temple' from *Modern Korean Poetry,* translated by Jaihiun Kim (1994), by permission of Asian Humanities Press, a division of Jain Publishing Company; **Gillian Clarke,** 'In the Barn' from *The Animal Wall,* Pont Books, Gomer Press (1999), by permission of the author; **Rita Dove,** 'Fifth Grade Autobiography' from *Grace Notes* by Rita Dove. Copyright © 1989 by Rita Dove, by permission of the author and W W Norton & Company, Inc; **V Elwin and S Hivale,** 'Love and Music' from *Folk Songs of the Maikal Hills* by V Elwin and S Hivale (1944), by permission of Oxford University Press, New Delhi, India; **Annette Mbaye d'Erneville,** 'My House' from *Talking Drums,* ed. Veronique Tadjo, A & C Black (2000), by permission of Les Nouvelles Editions Africaines du Senegal; **Nizzim Ezekiel,** 'Touching' from *Latter-Day Psalms* by Nizzim Ezekiel, by permission of Oxford University Press, New Delhi, India; **Nikki Giovanni,** 'Trips' from *Spin a Soft Black Song* by Nikki Giovanni. Copyright " 1975, 1985 by Nikki Giovanni, by permission of Hill and Wang, a division of Farrar, Straus and Giroux, LLC; **Luigi Grossi,** 'The Town Factory'('La Fabbrica delle città') from *E' arrivato un bastimento . . .,* (1998), by permission of Edizioni EL; **Lance Henson,** 'Sundown at Darlington 1878' from *Voices of the Rainbow,* edited by Kenneth Rosen. Copyright © 1973, 1993 by Kenneth Rosen, by permission of Seaver Books; **Langston Hughes,** 'I, Too, Sing America' from *The Collected Poems of Langston Hughes.* Copyright © 1994 by the Estate of Langston Hughes, by permission of David Higham Associates on behalf of the Estate of the author and Alfred A Knopf Inc, a division of Random House, Inc; **Miroslav Holub,** 'The Door' from *Selected Poems: Miroslav Holub,* translated by Ian Milner and George Theiner, Penguin Books (1967), p. 62. Copyright © Miroslav Holub 1967, by permission of Penguin Books Ltd; **Bizhan Jalâli,** 'With Their Fingers', first published in *Modern Persian Poetry,* edited and translated by Mahmud Kianush (1996), by permission of The Rockingham Press; **Jenny Joseph,** 'Going Out With Mum' from *All the Things I See* by Jenny Joseph, Macmillan (2000), by permission of John Johnson Ltd on behalf of the author; **Jackie Kay,** 'Two Carla Johnsons' from *Two's Company* by Jackie Kay, Blackie, (1992) p. 11. Copyright © Jackie Kay 1992, by permission of Penguin Books Ltd; **Kirsi Kunnas,** 'The Pan and the Potatoes' from *The Tumpkin's Wonder Tree/Tätiäsen Satupuu* (1956), by permission of Werner Söderström Corporation; **Harold Littlebird,** 'Could I Say I Touched You' from *Voices of the Rainbow,* edited by Kenneth Rosen (1973). Copyright © 1973, 1993 by Kenneth Rosen, by permission of Seaver Books; **John Montague,** 'What a View' from *Collected Poems* by John Montague (1995), by permission of the author, The Gallery Press and Wake Forest University Press; **Christian Morgenstern,** 'The Scarecrow' from *Lullabies, Lyrics and Gallows Songs,* selected by Lisbeth Zwerger (1995), by permission of Nord-Sud Verlag AG; **Senke Motomaro,** 'Secret' from *Burning Giraffes,* edited and translated by James Kirkup, University of Salzburg Press (1996), by permission of James Kirkup; **Nader Naderpur,** 'Morning Song', first published in *Modern Persian Poetry,* edited and translated by Mahmud Kianush (1996), by permission of The Rockingham Press; **Stella Ngatho,** 'Footpath', included in *Poems from East Africa,* eds. David Cook and David Rubadiri (1971), by permission of East African Educational Publishers Ltd; **Grace Nichols,** 'Sea Timeless Song' from *Come Into My Tropical Garden,* A & C Black (1988). Copyright © Grace Nichols 1988, by permission of Curtis Brown Ltd on behalf of the author; **Sigbjørn Obstfelder,** 'Rain' ('Regn') translated by Sarah Hails. English translation copyright © world rights 2001, Sandvik AS, by permission of Sandvik AS Norway; **Frank O'Hara,** 'Autobiographia Literaria' from *The Collected Poems of Frank O'Hara.* Copyright © 1971 by Maureen Granville-Smith, Administratrix of the Estate of Frank O'Hara, by permission of Alfred A Knopf, a division of Random House, Inc; **Brian Patten,** 'Dear Mum' from *Thawing Frozen Frogs,* Viking. Copyright © Brian Patten 1990, by permission of Rogers, Coleridge and White on behalf of the author; **Andrew Fusek Peters,** 'Chant for a Child Who is Hurt', translated by Andrew Fusek Peters and Malle Burggraf, included in *Sheep Don't Go to School,* Bloodaxe Books (1999), by permission of Andrew Fusek Peters; **Michael Rosen,** 'Busy Day' from *You Tell Me* by Michael Rosen and Roger McGough, Puffin (1979), by permission of The Peters Fraser and Dunlop Group Ltd on behalf of the author; **Sennur Sezer,** 'Morning Song', first published in *Modern Turkish Poetry,* edited and translated by Feyyaz Kayacan Fergar (1992), by permission of The Rockingham Press; **Edith Södergran,** 'The Stars' from *Complete Poems* by Edith Södergran, translated by David McDuff (1984), by permission of Bloodaxe Books; **Marin Sorescu,** 'Playing Icarus' from *The Biggest Egg in the World* by Marin Sorescu, (1987), by permission of Bloodaxe Books; **Matthew Sweeney,** 'All the Dogs' from *The Flying Spring Onion* by Matthew Sweeney (1992), by permission of Faber and Faber Ltd; **Rabindranath Tagore,** 'Paper Boats' from *The Crescent Moon* by Rabindranath Tagore, by permission of Visva-Bharati University, Calcutta; **Marina Tsvetaeva,** 'A Kiss on the Head', translated by Elaine Feinstein, from *Selected Poems* by Elaine Feinstein (1993), by permission of Carcanet Press Ltd; **Andrei Voznesensky,** 'Bicycles' from *Selected Poems of Andrei Voznesensky,* translated by Anselm Hollo (1964). Copyright © 1964 by Grove Press, by permission of Grove/Atlantic, Inc; **Albert Wendt,** 'Flying Foxes', included in *Ten Modern New Zealand Poets,* chosen by Harvey McQueen and Lois Cox (1974), by permission of the author; **Siv Widerberg,** 'Nightmare' from *I'm Like Me* by Siv Widerberg, translated by Verne Moberg. Copyright © 1968, 1969, 1970, 1971 by Siv Widerberg, translation copyright © 1973 by Verne Moberg, by permission of The Feminist Press at The City University of New York; **Jim Wong-Chu,** 'Ice' from *Chinatown Ghosts* (1986), by permission of Arsenal Pulp Press, Vancouver; **Judith Wright,** 'Night Herons' from *A Human Pattern: Selected Poems* by Judith Wright (1999), by permission of ETT Imprint, Sydney; **Han, Yong-un,** 'The Ferryboat and the Traveller' from *Modern Korean Poetry,* translated by Jaihiun Kim (1994), by permission of Asian Humanities Press, a division of Jain Publishing Company; **Kinoshita Yūji,** 'Voice and Wings' from *Burning Giraffes,* edited and translated by James Kirkup, University of Salzburg Press (1996), by permission of James Kirkup.

Every effort has been made to trace the copyright holders but if any have been inadvertently overlooked the publishers will be pleased to make the necessary arrangement at the first opportunity.